The Scientist's
Guide to Physics™

Discovering
Relativity

CORONA BREZINA

ROSEN
PUBLISHING®

New York

Published in 2015 by The Rosen Publishing Group, Inc.
29 East 21st Street, New York, NY 10010

Library of Congress Cataloging-in-Publication Data

Brezina, Corona.
Discovering relativity/Corona Brezina.—First edition.
     pages cm.—(The scientist's guide to physics)
Includes bibliographical references and index.
ISBN 978-1-4777-8006-0 (library bound)
1. General relativity (Physics)—Juvenile literature. I. Title.
QC173.6.B74 2015
530.11—dc23

                                                    2014019697

Manufactured in China

Contents

Introduction 4

CHAPTER 1   Before Relativity 8

CHAPTER 2   Einstein's Early Years 20

CHAPTER 3   Special Relativity 32

CHAPTER 4   General Relativity 46

CHAPTER 5   General Relativity and the
Cosmos 63

CHAPTER 6   Putting Relativity to the Test ... 79

Timeline 96

Glossary 98

For More Information 100

For Further Reading 103

Bibliography 105

Index 108

INTRODUCTION

In 1919, two teams of British astronomers traveled near the equator to observe a solar eclipse. Today, it's easy to view their historic expedition as a scientific excursion of an earlier, slower age. The groups traveled across the Atlantic Ocean by ship. After they took photographs, they had to wait for months to see the results while the photographic plates were sent back to England and developed. But the scientists had a very modern purpose in mind. They hoped that their observations would serve as proof of Albert Einstein's general theory of relativity.

The result of their work was a photo showing a slight shift in a group of stars relative to their position in another photo. But the slight bending of light ushered in a new way of understanding the universe. The photos demonstrated that the sun's gravitational field curved the fabric of space-time. It was confirmation of the validity of Einstein's general theory of relativity, his greatest achievement and, today, one of the landmark theories of science. In Andrew Robinson's book *Einstein: A Hundred Years of Relativity*, the renowned physicist Stephen Hawking states that the general theory of relativity "spurred the greatest change in our perception of the universe in which we live since Euclid wrote his *Elements of Geometry* around 300 BC."

Einstein, then a professor of physics in Berlin, was already highly regarded by his scientific peers. The eclipse experiment brought international recognition to Einstein and his work. Newspapers around the world hailed relativity as a revolution in science. Einstein himself became instantly famous.

The popularity of Einstein and relativity, however, did not mean that the general public understood his work. Following the successful observation of the eclipse, the expedition's leader, Arthur Eddington, was honored at the official announcement. A colleague complimented Eddington on his accomplishment, commenting that he was probably one of only three men in the world who understood

An April 27, 1919, photograph taken in Brazil shows the instruments Eddington's expedition used to observe the solar eclipse. Movable mirrors directed images of the sun into two horizontal telescopes.

Einstein's theory. Eddington remained silent, and the colleague urged him not to be modest. Eddington replied that on the contrary, he was trying to think of who the third might be.

Einstein's general theory of relativity, published in 1915, was the product of more than a decade of work on relativity. He had begun by considering a limited approach to the subject, which is now called special relativity. Einstein's special theory of relativity, however, also made mind-boggling revisions to the laws of physics. Time and space were not absolute. Time and space were relative. In an afterthought to the theory, Einstein stated that matter and energy were interchangeable. Later, in his general theory of relativity, he described how gravitational fields affect the curvature of space-time.

Today, Einstein is still recognized as the personification of eccentric genius. His theory of relativity also endures as a framework for understanding how the universe works. General relativity predicted the existence of black holes when even Einstein refused to believe in their reality. General relativity remains valid in a universe in which objects are moving apart at an accelerating rate, a phenomenon that even Einstein never predicted. A hundred years after Einstein published his general theory of relativity, it still underpins new breakthroughs occurring in science.

BEFORE RELATIVITY

Chapter

1

lbert Einstein was born during an era in which scientists' understanding of physics was undergoing an unprecedented transformation. At the cusp of the twentieth century, astronomers did not know of the existence of galaxies other than the Milky Way. Physicists were not convinced that matter was made up of atoms. Scientists believed that space was infused by a mysterious material called ether. By the time of Einstein's death in 1955, scientists had shown that humans live in an expanding universe made up of many galaxies. The world had seen the creation of the atomic bomb.

Late in his life, Einstein wrote about how he developed "suspicion against every kind of authority" as a child, as quoted in Robinson's *Einstein: A Hundred Years of Relativity*. He described his "sceptical attitude towards the convictions which were alive in any specific social environment—an attitude which has never again left me." Einstein's cynical outlook led to groundbreaking new ideas across the field of physics, the best known being his theories of relativity that reshaped the framework of physics and changed the way scientists study the universe. Einstein achieved his unprecedented scientific breakthroughs through independent thinking and a willingness to challenge conventional wisdom, even when conventional wisdom consisted of revered scientific principles that had remained unchallenged for centuries.

CLASSICAL PHYSICS

The concept of relativity is strongly associated with Einstein, yet the idea did not originate with him. Relativity of motion was first described by Galileo Galilei in 1632. Best remembered today for his work in astronomy, Galileo is sometimes referred to as the father of modern science.

Galileo described relativity using the example of a ship traveling in a straight line at a constant speed. Although the ship and its contents are

Galileo is credited with developing the modern scientific method. He held that physics should be studied through experimentation and mathematical description.

in motion, the ship's motion does not affect the motions of objects on the ship. Imagine tossing a ball, pouring water, jumping up and down, or conducting a physics experiment relating to motion. The laws of motion yield the same results whether the ship itself is in motion or at rest. That is because the contents are moving at the same rate as the ship.

The detection of motion depends on the observer's frame of reference. To an observer on the ship who is not looking outside a window, the ship seems to be at rest. To an observer on land, the ship is obviously in motion. Therefore, motion is relative. An object's motion can only be observed in relation to another object.

Although Galileo had established that motion is relative, the principles governing motion were still not fully understood. In his day, the laws of physics

Galileo used a thought experiment involving a smoothly sailing ship to describe his principle of relativity. Today, many science books use the example of an airplane cruising at high speed.

could not explain why, for example, an object thrown into the air fell in a parabolic trajectory. Isaac Newton emerged to bring order to the field. His 1687 work, *Principia*, set forth three laws governing motion.

Newton based his theories of motion on forces. A force is the push or pull that occurs when one object interacts with another. Newton's three laws established mathematical equations that described objects in motion. His first law stated that an object

Newton's universal law of gravitation
explains the motion of bodies in space
as well as the effects of gravity on
objects on earth.

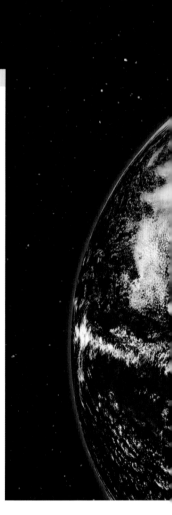

in motion would stay in motion, and an object at rest would remain at rest, unless acted upon by an outside force. The second law, which deals with acceleration, describes the amount of force that must be applied to move an object. The third law states that for every action, there is an equal and opposite reaction.

Newton also formulated a universal law of gravitation. He proposed that all objects are subject to the force of gravity. Two objects exert a gravitational attraction upon each other, the strength of the attraction depending on the objects' masses and the distance between them.

Newton's laws applied to objects in space as well as on Earth. The universal law of gravitation, in particular, resolved many unanswered questions about the nature of the cosmos. Heavenly bodies exerted gravitational forces on each other. Gravity

explained why the moon circled around Earth. Newton's laws predicted the planets' speed and shape of their orbits.

Newton's laws of motion described an orderly, mechanical universe. Time was constant, space was

TWO GENIUSES

Who was the greater genius—Albert Einstein or Isaac Newton (1642–1727)? Discussion of the question unfailingly ends in a draw, but interesting parallels exist between them. Both achieved impressive work in multiple disciplines—Newton made breakthroughs in optics, mathematics, and chemistry as well as in physics. Both, however, are associated primarily with their work in physics that redefined the framework of the universe. Newton described the laws of classical physics that Einstein overturned when he developed relativity. Both had a particularly productive "miracle year" when they were young. Newton made revolutionary breakthroughs in optics, calculus, and physics in the year spanning 1665 and 1666; Einstein's miracle year was 1905. They both became known for their activities outside science. Newton served as a member of Parliament and as master of the Royal Mint. Einstein championed causes such as world peace, freedom of expression, and civil rights.

unchanging, and matter could be neither created nor destroyed. This mechanistic view remained unquestioned for centuries.

THE NATURE OF LIGHT

In the late nineteenth century, as scientists explored the physics of light, magnetism, and electricity, they found that Newton's physics failed to explain some of their observations. Newton had done groundbreaking work in optics, but he did not understand the nature of light. He believed that light was a stream of particles. During the nineteenth century, some physicists proposed that light was actually a wave.

Early researchers working with electricity and magnetism realized that the two phenomena were related. Electricity and magnetism exert effects through fields, not through Newton's forces. Scientists found that an electric current could create a magnetic field. The opposite was also true. An electric current could be induced by a changing magnetic field.

A physicist named James Clerk Maxwell solved the conundrum of how electricity and magnetism were linked. He observed that for fields, unlike forces, time was a contributing factor in their effects.

Fields do not act instantaneously. Picture a magnet surrounded by iron filings. The filings are gradually attracted and repelled by the magnet's poles as they move to reveal the shape of the magnetic field. Fields, unlike forces, could be described as moving at a particular speed.

Maxwell developed the groundbreaking concept of combining electric and magnetic fields to create an electromagnetic wave. He described the results in four famous equations, today known simply as "Maxwell's equations." The electromagnetic wave was a result of the changing electric field generating a magnetic field and vice versa.

Maxwell was able to calculate the speed of his electromagnetic wave. He found that the speed was the same as the speed of light, which had been measured experimentally. Therefore, Maxwell had demonstrated that light was a wave. To be precise, it was an electromagnetic wave.

Maxwell's breakthrough, however, still did not fully solve the nature of light. It did not, for instance, explain how light moved through space. Scientists did not believe that light could travel in

When iron filings are brought within a magnetic field, they rearrange themselves to reveal the pattern of the field, clustering in the areas where the field is strongest.

a vacuum. They hypothesized that space was permeated by a substance they called ether, and that this medium allowed for the transmission of light. But ether was believed to be weightless and transparent, and its existence had never been proven.

In 1887, two scientists, Albert Michelson and Edward Morley, designed an experiment to detect the presence of ether. They built an optical device called an interferometer that split a beam of light using a mirror. The two beams, oriented at right angles to each other, were then recombined. If the two split beams had traveled at different speeds before being recombined, the apparatus would register interference—one wave pattern would shift slightly relative to the other.

Michelson and Morley believed that as Earth rotated and moved around the sun, its motion would result in an ether wind. They expected that since the split beams were traveling in different directions relative to the ether, the ether wind would have a different effect on each. One beam would be moving slightly more slowly than the other when the beam recombined. They hoped that their interferometer would be able to detect the effects of this ether wind.

Their sensitive and sophisticated apparatus, however, registered no interference pattern. No matter

Michelson and Morley's interferometer failed to detect the existence of ether in the universe, but the negative experimental result produced a landmark breakthrough in science.

how many times Michelson and Morley repeated the experiment, they never found any interference, meaning that they failed to detect the existence of ether. Their work cast doubt on the concept of ether flowing throughout the entire universe. Since the two light beams never exhibited interference, the experiment also demonstrated that the speed of light is constant.

EINSTEIN'S EARLY YEARS

Chapter

2

Albert Einstein was born in 1879 in the German town of Ulm. When he was still a baby, his family moved to Munich so that Einstein's father could join his brother's gas and electrical manufacturing company. Electric lighting, motors, generators, and other devices were still cutting-edge technology at the time. Einstein grew up tinkering with the contraptions, many of them experimental, related to the family business.

Einstein's father and uncle designed and improved new electrical inventions. One novel nineteenth-century invention was the magnetoelectric motor, in which magnetism produces an electric current.

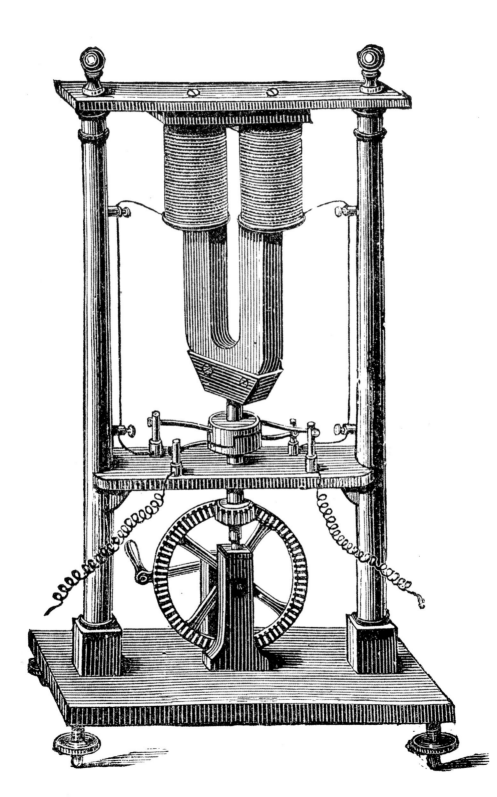

Einstein performed decently in school, excelling in math and physics. According to an often-repeated anecdote, Einstein failed math as a student, but it's untrue. He was so fascinated by advanced mathematics that he pored over math texts in his spare time and mastered advanced concepts, such as calculus, as a teenager. Nevertheless, he did not have an exemplary record as a student. Einstein was creative and nonconformist, and he had a natural suspicion of authority. He did not deal well with rote learning. Some of his teachers regarded him as cheeky.

After the family business failed, Einstein left school early without receiving a diploma, but he eventually finished his education in Switzerland. In 1896, he started classes at the Zurich Polytechnic Institute to study physics and math. Einstein felt that his courses focused too much on classical physics rather than new theories transforming the field, and his unorthodox and independent methods alienated some of the faculty.

Even as a student, Einstein expressed interest in the very aspects in physics that he would later revolutionize. At age sixteen, he wrote his first essay, entitled "On the Investigation of the State of the Ether in a Magnetic Field." For his graduation research thesis, he proposed building a machine that would split a beam of light so that each would travel a different direction relative to Earth's motion. At that point, he was unaware of Michelson and Morley's similar experiment. Einstein's instructor rejected the idea.

After graduating in 1900, Einstein had trouble finding a job, partly because he lacked recommendations from his professors. He applied for teaching and academic positions but received no offers. His personal life was also uncertain. Einstein had taken up with a fellow physics student named Mileva Marić at the Polytechnic, and his parents did not approve. Their relationship continued after his graduation, although Marić failed her final exams and did not receive a diploma. For two years, Einstein earned a precarious living through temporary teaching and tutoring positions. In 1902, however, a friend arranged a job in a patent office for him. Einstein settled in to work as a technical expert, third class, in Bern, Switzerland.

EINSTEIN'S FIRST WORK

In his new job at the Swiss patent office, Einstein worked eight-hour days at his desk six days a week. Despite the long hours and the nonacademic setting, Einstein thrived as a scientist during the seven years he spent at the patent office. He could often finish up his reviewing and reporting of patent applications quickly enough to leave time for working on his own ideas later in the day.

Einstein enjoyed his work at the patent office. The patent applications he examined included a wide variety of inventions, including many that involved cutting-edge concepts in electromagnetism. In assessing a patent application, Einstein had to look beyond the surface details to analyze the underlying theoretical principles of the device. His boss encouraged him to challenge obvious assumptions and view the patent applications with a highly critical eye. His situation at the patent office also allowed Einstein intellectual freedom to develop his theories—in an academic position, he would probably have been constrained to respect prevailing scientific conventions rather than develop his groundbreaking ideas that revolutionized physics.

Einstein had kept abreast of the latest breakthroughs in physics since graduating from the Polytechnic. After arriving in Bern, he began holding informal evening study sessions with a couple friends who shared his interests in physics and philosophy. His friends provided Einstein with intellectual stimulation and helped him develop the philosophical framework that would serve as a foundation for his scientific explorations.

His stable job at the patent office allowed Einstein to settle down with Mileva Marić and start a family. They married in 1903, and she had a son in 1904.

Einstein poses with his wife, Mileva Marić, who pursued her studies in math and physics during a time when the fields were overwhelmingly dominated by men.

THE "MIRACLE YEAR"

In spring 1905, writing to a friend, Einstein announced that he was planning to publish four papers that year. He described the topics, which each addressed different fundamental aspects of physics. Einstein ultimately exceeded his own ambitious expectations. Three of the papers were so revolutionary that each alone would have established Einstein's legacy in physics. As an afterthought, Einstein published a fifth paper that introduced the most famous equation in science: $E = mc^2$. Some people have described the six months in which he wrote these papers as the most notable period of productivity for a scientist at any point in history. All of his papers were published in the leading German physics journal of the day.

Mileva Marić read over his papers before Einstein submitted them for publication. Some journalists have speculated on the extent of Marić's contributions to her husband's work. Marić herself never took any credit for any of Einstein's groundbreaking concepts, however, and no evidence exists that any of Einstein's ideas originated with his wife.

The first paper, completed in March, put forth a new theory on the nature of light. It explained an experimental phenomenon called the photoelectric effect. Under certain circumstances, when a light beam struck a metal surface, it resulted in an electron being ejected. Most scientists believed light to be a wave, yet the photoelectric effect was not consistent with the wave theory. In 1900, a physicist named Max Planck had proposed that energy existed in discrete bundles called quanta. Einstein extended Planck's concept to light, proposing that light itself was composed of energy quanta (later called photons) that could be represented as a wave. When a photon strikes a metal surface, it transfers its energy to an electron in the metal and causes it to be ejected. Einstein's quantum theory of light eventually became one of the foundations of the field of quantum mechanics, which overturned Newton's mechanistic portrayal of the universe.

In April, Einstein completed a paper that he later submitted to the University of Zurich as his doctoral dissertation. Entitled "A New Determination of Molecular Dimensions," it established the size of sugar molecules by examining their behavior in water. Although it was not as transformative as his other 1905 papers, it yielded many practical applications and therefore is often cited in other scientific articles. It also earned Einstein his Ph.D.

Einstein's May paper, which drew on some of the concepts put forth in his dissertation, examined a phenomenon called Brownian motion. In 1828, a botanist named Robert Brown had observed with a microscope that particles suspended in a liquid tend to move around in random zigzags. Scientists could not explain the movements. The existence of atoms was still speculative, and most physicists believed that in any case, the atoms making up water molecules would be too small to affect the comparatively huge suspended particles. Einstein determined that masses of molecules moving at random could affect the motion of a suspended particle when

they temporarily shifted in a particular direction. He provided calculations to prove his theory, including the dimensions of atoms. With his analysis, Einstein provided evidence supporting the existence of atoms. His work on Brownian motion also marked

These sugar crystals are lit by bright colored lights. Although less innovative than his later work, Einstein's doctoral thesis broke new ground by measuring sizes of molecules, such as sugar, in liquids.

a breakthrough in applying statistical methods to problems in physics. His predictions were later confirmed in the lab.

THE THEORETICAL PHYSICIST

Einstein worked as a theoretical physicist, not as an experimentalist. His work consisted of new ideas that drew on existing scientific and philosophical principles. Einstein did not attempt to prove the validity of his theories with experiments, nor did he draw extensively on experimental findings.

Unlike the scientists who hoped for decisive results in their experiments and analyses, Einstein enjoyed exploring contradictions. In much of his work, he

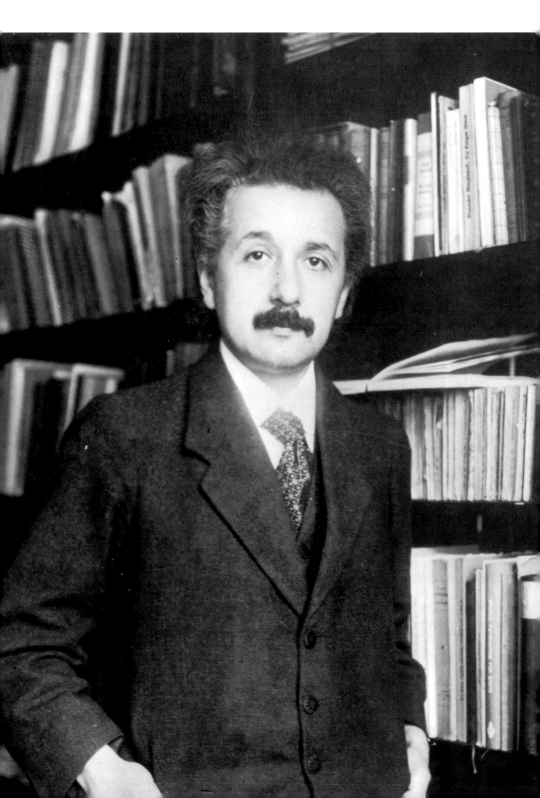

attempted to resolve contradictions between theoretical predictions and experimental results or refine theories that contained inconsistencies. In *Einstein: His Life and Universe*, Walter Isaacson points out that Einstein tended to use a deductive approach in describing his theories. In his three groundbreaking 1905 papers, he began by stating certain postulates, or basic assumptions relevant to the problem. He then derived certain conclusions from these postulates, formulating his own theory that resolved the contradictions among existing theories on the topic.

In 1905, the twenty-six-year-old patent clerk Albert Einstein made a series of breakthroughs that forever transformed the field of physics.

SPECIAL RELATIVITY

Chapter
3

I mmediately following its publication, Einstein and many of his colleagues considered his March paper on the nature of light to be the most influential of his 1905 works. But his paper completed in June, "On the Electrodynamics of Moving Bodies," addressed relativity, the topic in physics that would become most closely linked to his name. This paper discussed special relativity, which dealt with the motion of two inertial frames of reference moving at a constant speed relative to each other. Einstein added the "special" qualifier years later to differentiate it from his general theory of relativity.

Einstein began by stating two postulates, or basic assumptions. The first was the principle of relativity established by Galileo, which stated that the laws of physics are the same in all inertial frames of reference. They would remain constant whether an observer was on a moving airplane or at rest. Einstein expanded the concept to include electromagnetic waves as well as the laws of motion.

His second postulate involved the speed of light, a topic that had fascinated him ever since he was sixteen years old. Young Albert had devised a thought experiment in which he imagined himself traveling alongside a beam of light. If he were moving at the speed of light, the beam of light should appear to be at rest. Yet according to Maxwell's equations, it was impossible for light to exist in a state of rest in any frame of reference. To Einstein, the situation presented a paradox.

Nonetheless, he put forth as his second postulate that the speed of light in a vacuum has the same value in all inertial frames of reference. This diverged with the ether theory that was still upheld by many scientists. They believed that light moved at a fixed speed relative to the ether—the mysterious medium that had never been detected experimentally.

Einstein now faced the challenge of reconciling two apparently incompatible postulates. How could the principle of relativity accommodate a constant speed of light? The difficulties can be illustrated with another thought experiment. Say that a beam

of light coming from a train is visible in several different observers—a stationary woman watching the beam, a man running toward the train, and a driver moving away in the same direction as the train. The speed of the observers relative to the train varies, in agreement with the principle of relativity, yet to every observer the speed of light emitted by the train remains constant.

Einstein resolved the discrepancy by reassessing the nature of time itself. According to Newton, time and space were absolute. Einstein concluded that time is relative. Time flows differently for every inertial frame of reference. For our experiences in everyday life, in which we do not experience relativistic effects, Newton's physics remain valid. At extremely high speeds nearing the speed of light, however, Newton's rules no longer apply.

Einstein's revelation about the nature of time occurred when he recognized "an inseparable connection between time and the signal velocity," as quoted in John S. Rigdon's *Einstein 1905*. This connection pertained to simultaneity. An observer in one inertial frame of reference may perceive two

Einstein used the example of moving trains in many of his thought experiments. The patent office where he worked was located near a train station and a famous clock tower.

events as occurring simultaneously. To an observer in an inertial frame of reference moving at a high rate of speed, however, one event may appear to occur before the other. For each inertial frame of reference, time is relative.

The concept of the relativity of time leads to the property of time dilation. The measured time that elapses between two events is different for observers in different inertial frames of reference. Einstein determined that for an observer moving at a higher rate of speed, time elapses more slowly. This property has been proven experimentally using two highly accurate clocks. One was sent to travel around the world on an airplane while the other stayed on the ground. When the two clocks were compared, the clock that had traveled at a high rate of speed was running slow by a tiny fraction of a second. For that clock, time had run more slowly while it traveled on the airplane at a high rate of speed.

Einstein's postulates and the property of time dilation led him to another conclusion. Space is also relative. Observers in different inertial frames of reference measuring the same distance will report different results. Einstein found that space is shortened for an observer moving at the higher rate of speed. This property is known as length contraction.

Length contraction is related to Einstein's observations on simultaneity. To measure a distance or length, the observer marks the start point and end point simultaneously. But as observed with time dilation, two events that are simultaneous for an observer at rest relative to the object being measured may not be simultaneous for an observer in motion. For the observer in motion, the physical distance between the start point and end point is shorter than for the observer at rest.

Einstein was not the first person to develop some of his concepts in special relativity. The French physicist and mathematician Henri Poincaré had considered the matter of relativity and questioned the nature of time. The Irish physicist George Francis FitzGerald had developed equations related to length contraction, and the Dutch physicist Hendrik Lorentz expanded on his work to include time dilation. None of them, however,

The Nobel Prize–winning physicist Hendrik Lorentz formulated the concept of the electron and developed the Lorentz transformations, which were relevant to special relativity.

were as bold as Einstein in redefining the foundations of physics.

Lorentz did not consider his equations to have any significance to the real world. Nonetheless, they could be applied to Einstein's special theory of relativity. The Lorentz transformations are the mathematical tools that are used to calculate the coordinates in different inertial frames of reference. Einstein credited Lorentz's work with helping him develop his special theory of relativity, and the two men later became close friends.

Implications of Special Relativity

The concepts of special relativity are often illustrated by a thought experiment called the twin paradox. Imagine that one twin departs on a spaceship traveling close to the speed of light. She travels to a planet several light-years distant, and then the spaceship turns around to return to Earth. When the twins are reunited, which one is older?

To the traveling twin, time moved more slowly during the journey. Therefore, the traveling twin should be younger than the stay-at-home twin upon returning.

The paradox arises, however, in considering the two frames of reference. Relative to Earth, the

The twin paradox is used to illustrate the concept that time is relative. Mathematical calculations can determine the precise age difference between the theoretical traveling twins.

twin on the spaceship moved away at a high rate of speed. But from the perspective of the twin on the spaceship, it appeared that Earth was moving away while the spaceship remained at rest, meaning that the stay-at-home twin should be younger. According to the principle of relativity, both frames of reference are valid.

The stay-at-home twin, however, remains in the same inertial frame of reference. Meanwhile, the traveling twin accelerates and slows during the course of the trip, which means that the twins do not share identical experiences during their separation relative to each other.

There have been many different explanations of the twin paradox using various arguments in special relativity. Alternate versions claim that the situation cannot be fully addressed by special relativity, which applies to objects at constant speed. In this case, the problem must be resolved by arguments in general relativity.

Einstein's paper on special relativity reached one final conclusion: it is not possible for an object in motion to reach the speed of light.

His explanation introduced the idea that mass is relative. The measured mass of an object that is at rest in its inertial frame of reference will not be the same as the measured mass of the same object that is in motion relative to its inertial frame of reference. The relativistic mass of the object in motion is larger at higher speeds, although the effect is not noticeable except at speeds close to the speed of light.

Imagine that a spaceship traveling at nearly the speed of light attempts to accelerate to the speed of light. Acceleration requires that a force be exerted to increase the speed—the equivalent of stepping on the spaceship's gas pedal. But as the speed is increased, the spaceship's relativistic mass increases, resisting acceleration. At the speed of light, the

PARTICLE ACCELERATORS

Physicists who work with particle accelerators deal with the implications of special relativity as part of the job. As their name indicates, particle accelerators accelerate sub-atomic particles to extremely high velocities, sometimes approaching the speed of light. Because of the high energy involved, the mass of the accelerated particles increases. When these particles collide, they sometimes create new, heavier particles as well as energy, giving physicists plenty of opportunities to use Einstein's $E = mc^2$ equation. Particle accelerators allow scientists to study the basic constituents of matter and how they interact.

In 2011, scientists at the massive European CERN (European Organization for Nuclear Research) particle accelerator claimed that they had observed neutrinos traveling faster than the speed of light, a finding that challenged Einstein's special theory of relativity. It later turned out that the result was an error due to a faulty cable connection.

Einstein referenced Isaac Newton and wrote out an equation for energy in one of his earliest surviving manuscripts on relativity.

object's relativistic mass would be infinite and would require an infinite force to accelerate it. Because there can be no such thing as an infinite force, the speed of light is the cosmic speed limit.

EINSTEIN'S FAMOUS EQUATION

In autumn 1905, Einstein wrote to a friend that he'd had an afterthought related to his paper on special relativity. "Namely, the relativity principle, together with Maxwell's equations, requires that mass be a direct measure of the energy contained in a body," as quoted in Walter Isaacson's *Einstein: His Life and Universe*. In September, he submitted the paper "Does the Inertia of a Body Depend on Its Energy Content?" for publication. It was only three pages long.

The root of the paper was the famous equation $E = mc^2$. Einstein summarized it by stating that "The mass of a body is a measure of its energy content," as quoted by Isaacson. In the equation, E represents the energy, m the mass of an object, and c the speed of light, which Einstein had established is constant.

As with his other 1905 papers, Einstein employed a deductive approach. He began, as mentioned in the letter, by considering Maxwell's theory and the principle of relativity. He opens the paper by summarizing his conclusions on special relativity, and the findings of the September paper represent a logical follow-up to his earlier work.

In the paper, Einstein presents the thought experiment of an object emitting light. Einstein applies the principles of relativity in considering the object observed in a stationary inertial frame of reference and in a moving inertial frame of reference. The energy of the light wave being emitted, represented by E, could have two sources, either a decrease in the velocity of the object or a decrease in the mass of the object. It cannot be possible that the velocity decreases, since one frame of reference is stationary. Therefore, the mass of the object must decrease, the lost amount of mass being converted into energy. With this simple chain of logic, Einstein demonstrated that matter and energy are fundamentally interchangeable.

Einstein altered the foundations of physics yet again with this conclusion. Classical physics had held that energy could be neither created nor destroyed.

Now, with Einstein's demonstration that energy and matter were interchangeable, matter had to be considered as well in the law of conservation.

Einstein suggested that his conclusions could be tested experimentally using radium, a radioactive element that emits energy. If his theory was correct, the mass of a sample of radium should decrease to account for the radioactive energy. As it turned out, at the time, the mass decrease was too small to detect in a lab.

Einstein's equation had significant practical implications. The speed of light, c, is a huge number—186,000 miles per second or 3 million meters per second. That number is squared mathematically—it is multiplied by itself—and then it is multiplied by the amount of mass, m. The result is a massive amount of energy, E. One gram of matter converted into energy would produce about 25 million kilowatt hours, which is more than enough electricity to power 25,000 homes for over a month.

GENERAL RELATIVITY

Chapter
4

Einstein's work on relativity would eventually make him the most famous physicist in the history of the world. But after his productive year of 1905, his colleagues were slow to recognize the significance of his work. Einstein had hoped for recognition in the academic community, and maybe even a job offer of a teaching position. Instead, he expressed disappointment that his publications failed to make an immediate impact.

He was incorrect in believing that his work had gone unnoticed. One of the most influential physicists of the day, Max Planck, took an interest in Einstein's paper on relativity. In 1906, Planck became the first scientist to support the theory of relativity in a published article.

With Planck backing Einstein's ideas, more physicists began taking relativity seriously. Nonetheless, Einstein's theories were too revolutionary to be accepted quickly. His highly theoretical approach required a new way of thinking about fundamental topics in physics, and many readers failed even to grasp his concepts at first. Once Einstein's theories became more widely circulated and discussed, they proved controversial and caused disagreement. Some scientists rejected relativity outright. Others were unwilling to accept some of Einstein's radical conclusions, such as the speed of light being constant or the fact that ether did not exist.

The Nobel Prize–winning physicist Max Planck revolutionized physics when he determined that energy was emitted in discrete bundles called quanta. Einstein proved that this applied to light, too.

Eventually, Einstein's work would elevate the entire field of theoretical physics to a new level of respect. In the meantime, Einstein completed his doctorate, received a promotion to technical expert, second class, and continued publishing papers on physics. In 1909, he finally became a professor, teaching physics at the University of Zurich in Switzerland.

TOWARD GENERAL RELATIVITY

Even as Einstein waited for a reaction to his work on relativity, he was already considering the limitations of his own theory. Special relativity applied only to objects in uniform motion. It did not pertain to objects that weren't moving in a straight line, nor could it be applied to objects that were accelerating. Einstein's special theory of relativity applied to various inertial frames of reference in which observers felt like they were at a state of rest relative to other frames of reference. Accelerated motion, by contrast, is not relative—a passenger in a vehicle can feel the effects of acceleration. Einstein began to contemplate whether it would be possible to "generalize" the concepts in his special theory of relativity.

In late 1907, Einstein had a sudden thought about the nature of gravity. A person in free fall would not feel his own weight. He would not be physically aware of the force of gravity. (Today, astronauts training for missions in space experience simulated weightlessness on a plane that nosedives from a high altitude.

During the brief period that the plane is falling, the passengers on the plane feel no tug of gravity.)

Einstein later described the moment of epiphany as the happiest thought of his life. His trivial observation about gravity put him on the course that would ultimately lead to his general theory of relativity, which applied to all motion.

But how was a property of gravity relevant to relativity? Einstein developed a principle of equivalence that explained the relationship between inertia, gravity, and acceleration. Later, the principle of equivalence became one of the cornerstones of his general theory of relativity.

Inertia is an object's resistance to a change in its state of motion—recall Newton's first law of motion. More force is required to roll a bowling ball across the floor than a tennis ball. The inertial mass of an object is a physical measure of its resistance to change in its state of motion. Physicists distinguished between inertial mass and gravitational mass, which is a measure of the gravitational force felt by the object. An object's inertial mass is not affected by gravity. The bowling ball has a larger inertial mass than the tennis ball whether it is on Earth or floating weightless in space.

Einstein concluded in his principle of equivalence that gravity is equivalent to accelerated motion. He used a thought experiment to illustrate his new idea. Imagine a man in a small, enclosed chamber. On Earth,

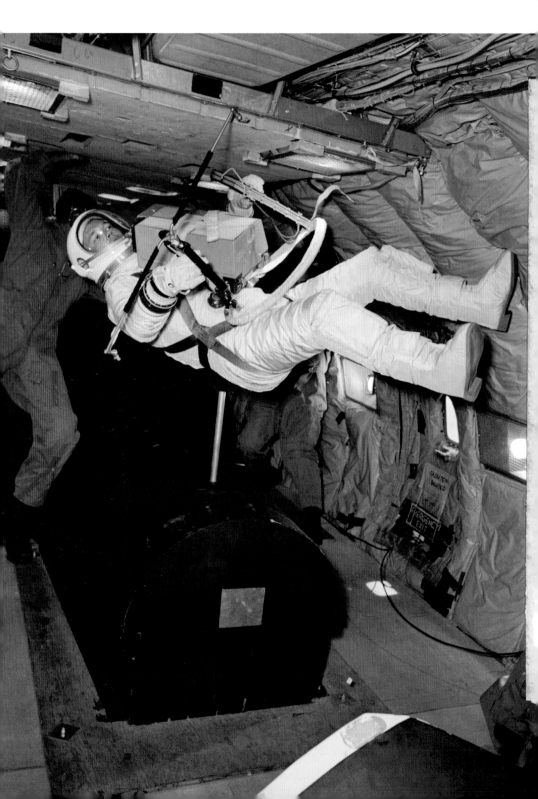

he would experience the force of gravity, which is 9.8 m/sec². If the chamber were floating through space, he would be weightless. But imagine that a rocket towed the chamber through space at an acceleration of 9.8 m/sec². The man would experience exactly the same conditions because of the acceleration through space as he experienced on Earth because of gravity.

The principle of equivalence also explains the relationship between inertial mass and gravitational mass. Before Einstein, physicists knew that inertial mass and gravitational mass had the same value. But they had never determined a scientific basis for this equivalence. The bowling ball and the tennis ball will both fall at the same rate, since they both experience an acceleration of 9.8 m/sec² due to the force of gravity. Yet objects with a greater gravitational mass experience a greater force of gravity—the bowling ball with a gravitational mass one hundred times larger than the tennis ball will experience one hundred times the gravitational force of the tennis ball. So why doesn't the bowling ball fall faster? The reason is that the bowling ball also has an inertial mass one hundred times larger, meaning that it

An astronaut undergoes training that simulates zero-gravity conditions on a military aircraft. For a period of about twenty-five seconds, as the plane is in free fall, passengers experience weightlessness.

takes one hundred times as much force to accelerate it into motion. The force exerted by gravity exactly counteracts the object's resistance to being accelerated, fulfilling Einstein's principle of equivalence. Therefore, inertial mass and gravitational mass are equivalent.

WORKING IN "SPACE-TIME"

After developing the principle of equivalence, Einstein took a break from relativity for three years while he focused on papers related to quantum physics. In 1911, he returned to expand on his theory of relativity. He quickly realized that the concepts behind general relativity required much more intensive mathematics than his work on special relativity.

Meanwhile, Einstein's theory had found approval from an unexpected source. Hermann Minkowski, a math professor at Zurich Polytechnic Institute, had taught Einstein as a student. Einstein had rarely attended class, and Minkowski considered him lazy. Minkowski was astonished that Einstein went on to produce the groundbreaking and elegant special theory of relativity.

Minkowski undertook to develop a formal mathematical interpretation of Einstein's theory. In 1908, he introduced the formulation of four-dimensional space-time. It incorporated the three physical dimensions as well as time, the fourth dimension. Minkowski's mathematics unified space and time into a space-time continuum. It described both position and motion and could be used to represent space-time events. Initially, Einstein thought that Minkowski's space-time structure was superfluous to his concepts of special relativity. Later, however, he found that the mathematics proved useful in dealing with moving reference frames in the general theory of relativity.

Hermann Minkowski provided mathematical tools for making calculations in four-dimensional space-time, which included the coordinates x, y, and z, and t for time.

As Einstein returned to his work on relativity, he found that traditional geometric tools could not be used to describe four-dimensional space-time. Euclidian geometry deals with flat planes and straight lines. Einstein required a geometry system that could be applied to curved surfaces and more than three dimensions.

Bernhard Riemann developed a type of geometry applicable to curved surfaces such as a sphere or four-dimensional space-time.

Einstein consulted a former classmate from Polytechnic who had studied non-Euclidean geometry extensively. His friend recommended the theoretical work of Bernhard Riemann, a nineteenth-century German mathematician. Riemann had developed a branch of geometry that dealt with curved surfaces. He considered his work to be purely abstract, with no relevance to physical reality. Einstein found that he could use Riemann's geometry to describe motion in curved space-time. Riemann's geometry provided the means of measuring the distance between two points in space regardless of how it curved. This involved complex mathematical tools called tensors. In Euclidian geometry, some physical quantities such as forces are represented by vectors, which have both magnitude and direction. Tensors are geometric entities that incorporate many more components than vectors.

UNDERSTANDING GRAVITY

One of the starting points in Einstein's development of his general theory of relativity was an unexplained aspect of Newton's theory of gravity. Newton's equations correctly predicted the effects of gravity, but Newton could not explain the mechanism of gravity. The force of gravity keeps the planets orbiting around the sun, for example, but how does the sun exert its force of attraction across the vast distances of the solar system? Newton described gravity as a force that acted instantaneously. Einstein was skeptical of the notion that gravity could reach out at a speed faster than that of light.

Einstein also began to speculate about the effect of gravity on light itself. In his earlier work, he had demonstrated that light contained energy and that energy and matter were interchangeable. Therefore, light should be affected by the force of gravity. The effect would only be measurable experimentally when light was affected by an extremely massive object. The gravitational field of the sun, for example, should bend light from distant stars. But because of the sun's own brightness, the effect would only be visible during a solar eclipse, when the moon obscured the face of the sun.

In such a case, the beam of light would be curved by the pull of gravity. What if the shape of space

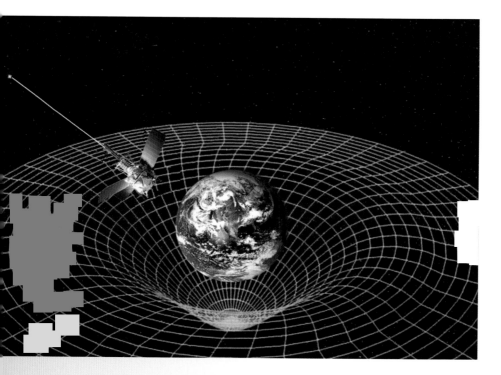

A probe is depicted orbiting Earth to test whether Einstein's general theory of relativity correctly predicts how the earth warps the local space-time around the planet.

itself, through which light traveled, was also affected by gravity? The question led to Einstein expanding the scope of his general theory of relativity. In addition to explaining how gravity works on objects, he wanted to figure out how gravitational fields cause space-time itself to curve.

Einstein's conception of curved four-dimensional space-time is impossible to visualize. As an analogy, imagine a trampoline with a bowling ball causing a depression in the center. The fabric of the trampoline is strained by the weight and no longer lies flat. Now imagine rolling a few marbles across the surface of the trampoline. They follow a curved path toward the bowling ball. The marbles aren't attracted to the bowling ball by some unseen force, as implied by Newton's conception of gravity. They move toward the bowling ball because it has changed the shape of the surrounding fabric of the trampoline. In the same way, the sun does not exert a pull on Earth. The sun's gravitational field causes space around it to curve, and the shape of space itself determines the movement of Earth.

Once Einstein had established his concept of gravity as curved space-time, he spent the next three years working on the mathematical equations for his theory. He started out with two principles, just as he had in developing special relativity. His first was the principle of equivalence, linking gravity and acceleration. The second he called the principle of covariance. It held that the laws of physics could be described by equations that hold true for all systems of coordinates. These "systems of coordinates" refer to the measurements of the space-time dimensions of frames of reference. Riemann's non-Euclidean geometry provided a means of describing curved space-times while fulfilling the principle of covariance.

RELATIVITY ON YOUR DASHBOARD

Einstein's theories of relativity provide indispensable tools for cosmologists and theoretical physicists, but they also have practical value. If scientists and engineers didn't understand special and general relativity, they would not have been able to develop the global positioning system (GPS). The receiver in the GPS device in a car determines location by detecting signals emitted by twenty-four satellites orbiting Earth at an altitude of 12,400 miles (20,000 kilometers) and moving at a speed of 8,700 miles per hour (14,000 kmph). The GPS device generally receives signals from at least four satellites, and the accuracy depends on the satellites highly precise atomic clocks agreeing on the time within twenty to thirty nanoseconds. However, special relativity predicts that the clocks traveling at high speeds relative to Earth will run slow. But general relativity predicts that because of the curvature of space-time around Earth, the satellites experience a weaker gravitational field than the surface of Earth, causing the clocks on the satellites to run fast. Therefore, the atomic clocks are automatically adjusted to compensate for the effects of relativity. Without this correction, GPS systems would fail within two minutes.

Eventually, Einstein succeeded in formulating a representation of space-time using this mathematical language. But he still had obstacles and wrong turns to overcome in his development of his general theory of relativity.

THE MERCURY DILEMMA

In 1912, Einstein devised an equation using a tensor that was close to his final mathematical description of space-time. But then he abandoned that approach to pursue an alternate strategy, believing that the results from his original version departed too drastically from Newton's laws. The next year, he published some of the alternate theory under the title, "Outline of a Generalized Theory of Relativity and a Theory of Gravitation." He was not completely satisfied with his own work, however, which did not adhere to his principle of covariance.

Einstein set out to test his theory on an unresolved conundrum of physics. In the nineteenth century, astronomers had noticed a small wobble in the orbit of the planet Mercury. The perihelion of Mercury's orbit—the point at which it passed closest to the sun—deviated slightly from Newton's predictions. Deviations in a planet's orbit were not unusual,

and they were usually explained by the effects of the gravitational fields of other planets. Some scientists believed that eventually, an unknown planet would be discovered that was affecting Mercury's orbit.

A more radical explanation was that the predictions made by Newton's laws were wrong. Einstein set out to test his "outline" theory on the Mercury problem. If his equations yielded the experimentally observed variation of Mercury's perihelion, it would prove his theory correct. But Einstein's results were not even close to the observed measurements. He continued to modify the "outline" approach until mid-1915, when he discovered several severe contradictions in the theory.

In late 1915, Einstein returned to the tensor analysis for a gravitational field that he had set aside in 1912. He embarked on a grueling month of work that yielded a revised set of equations. In November 1915, he tested his final theory by applying his calculations to Mercury's orbit. His equations yielded a figure that closely matched experimental observations. Later that month, he presented the set of equations for gravitational

In the nineteenth century, some astronomers believed that a mysterious planet called Vulcan caused the wobble in Mercury's orbit. Einstein's theory of general relativity resolved the puzzle.

fields at a lecture that marked the introduction of his theory to the world.

Einstein's equations are too complicated for anybody but math and physics experts to understand. Here is one version of his conception of curved space-time, as shown in Isaacson's *Einstein*:

$$R_{\mu\nu} - \tfrac{1}{2}g_{\mu\nu}R = 8\pi T_{\mu\nu}$$

The left-hand side of the equation describes the shape of space-time. The right-hand side describes the motion of matter.

Einstein was finally satisfied with his own theory, which has withstood the test of time. Today, the general theory of relativity is considered one of the milestones in the history of science.

GENERAL RELATIVITY AND THE COSMOS

Chapter 5

E instein completed his general theory of relativity while World War I (1914–1918) was still raging in Europe. As a lifelong pacifist, Einstein was horrified by the war. He also demonstrated his willingness to go against the tide of prevailing opinion in political and ideological matters as much as in his scientific work. Einstein had moved to Berlin in 1914, and many of his German scientific colleagues signed a manifesto supporting the war effort. Einstein refused to sign the document and contributed to a pacifist manifesto countering their viewpoint.

The war and problems in his marriage to Mileva Marić took a toll on Einstein's health. In 1917, suffering from stomach ailments, he lost more than fifty pounds (23 kilograms). He and Marić divorced in 1918, and Einstein married a cousin, Elsa Löwenthal, in 1919.

After completing his theoretical work on relativity in 1916, Einstein compiled his findings in a paper titled "The Foundation of the General Theory of Relativity." The journal that had published his 1905 papers issued it as a short standalone book. Einstein also wrote a book called *Relativity: The Special and the General Theory.* He intended this volume, a simplified version of his ideas, to introduce his theories to the general public. Einstein also continued to explore the ramifications of general relativity, which raised many questions about the nature of the universe. In some cases, it led to possibilities—such as the existence of black holes or the idea of an expanding universe—that Einstein himself found hard to believe.

The solar eclipse of 1919 allowed Einstein, at last, to verify with experimental data his prediction that the sun's gravitational field caused light to bend. The measurements demonstrated to the scientific world the validity of Einstein's general theory of relativity. It also had the less expected result of turning Einstein himself into an international celebrity.

LARGE-SCALE SCIENCE

Einstein's general theory of relativity involved ground-breaking applications of complex mathematics, but Einstein remained at heart a physicist. He did not pursue the mathematic concepts behind relativity for their own sake. His goal in developing his equations was to relate them to the principles of physics.

As he worked on the mathematics of relativity, Einstein double-checked whether or not his theoretical equations matched the laws of physics. The results had to adhere to the principle of equivalence, which linked gravity and acceleration. In most cases, they should obey the laws of classical physics. For weak gravitational fields—such as the gravity experienced on Earth—the results should agree with Newton's theory of gravity. Newton's laws failed only in extreme situations, when dealing with speeds approaching the speed of light.

After completing his general theory of relativity in 1915, Einstein moved on to study some of the implications of his work. Compared to special relativity, in which ideas could be conveyed by thought experiments involving trains and boats moving at different rates, general relativity was abstract and inaccessible, its effects apparent only on huge bodies in space. The equations of general relativity were relevant mainly to physics and advanced geometry. In addition, the general theory of relativity contributed to the development of an entire new discipline of science known as cosmology, which studies the origins and history of the universe.

In 1917, Einstein attempted to apply his general theory of relativity to the structure of space-time of the entire universe. It was the first time that anyone had tried to create a model of the universe. At the time, scientists believed that the universe was static— it was unmoving and had always existed in the same state. The universe was homogenous, meaning that it consisted of the same density of material throughout. Einstein conceived of a universe that was finite, not infinite, yet had no boundaries. At the edges of the universe, space-time would curve back on itself.

Einstein's equations, however, refused to adhere to the proposition that the universe was unmoving and unchanging. His calculations predicted that a static universe was impossible. The interactions of gravitational fields would force the universe to expand or contract. Either scientists' conception of the universe was incorrect or the equations of general relativity were wrong.

Despite his usual faith in his work, Einstein could not bring himself to believe in a potentially unstable universe. He modified his equations to fit the model of a static universe by incorporating an adjustment factor that he called a cosmological constant. He described the cosmological constant as imparting a counterbalance to the effect of gravity. Instead of attracting objects to each other, this element would cause repulsion. Therefore, it would cancel out the gravitational effects that would otherwise threaten to destabilize the universe.

Einstein published his conclusions in a paper titled "Cosmological Considerations in the General Theory of Relativity." A decade later, however, he would declare that the cosmological constant was the biggest mistake of his life.

Black Holes

The expanding universe wasn't the only prediction made by the general theory of relativity that Einstein found hard to believe. The general theory of relativity provided new tools for understanding the cosmos. It could predict the movement, interactions, and evolution of celestial bodies.

One of the earliest devotees of Einstein's theory was the mathematician and astrophysicist Karl Schwarzschild, who read about the theory while fighting in the German army on the Russian front. Schwarzschild briefly corresponded with

Einstein about general relativity before he died in mid-1916.

Einstein and Schwarzschild worked together to apply relativity to celestial bodies. Schwarzschild began by sending Einstein a description of a gravitational field surrounding a star. Einstein himself had used only approximations in testing his highly complex equations, so Schwarzschild's calculations of the curvature of space-time around a star provided the first exact solution to Einstein's equations. Schwarzschild then sent Einstein the calculations for the geometry of space-time inside a star.

Schwarzschild's calculations revealed an odd property of celestial bodies. Near the very center, the calculations for distance, space, and time stopped making sense. Schwarzschild found that once the mass of a star was compressed into a small enough sphere, it could become what is now known as a black hole. The size of the sphere—defined by a length called the Schwarzschild radius—depended only on the mass of the object. The radius for the sun, for example is 432,000 miles (696,000 km), and its Schwarzschild radius is a mere 1.9 miles (3 km).

Mathematician and astrophysicist Karl Schwarzschild applied the theory of general relativity to objects in space. In solving Einstein's field equations, he developed the concept of a black hole.

If the entire mass of the sun were compressed into a sphere with a radius of 1.9 miles (3 km), it would become a black hole so dense that light could not escape its gravitational field. Theoretically, any object could become a black hole if shrunk below its specific Schwarzschild radius.

The concept of a black hole had been proposed long before by the eighteenth-century scientist John Michell, who wrote of theoretical "dark stars." Like Newton, he conceived of light as consisting of tiny particles. Michell speculated on whether a star could exert a gravitational field so strong that it would exceed the escape velocity of light. Using Newton's law of gravity, he calculated that such a star would have to be small and dense. He found that a star with the mass of the sun would have a radius of 1.9 miles (3 km)—the same value calculated by Schwarzschild.

Black holes were originally called Schwarzschild singularities. The outside limit of the black hole, a sphere surrounding the Schwarzschild radius, is called the event horizon. Inside, matter is concentrated into a small point called a singularity, at which the laws of physics break down.

Einstein considered the Schwarzschild radius a theoretical concept that had no relevance in physical reality. In the 1930s, he argued that black holes could not exist because his calculations showed that particles would have to move at speeds exceeding the

EINSTEIN AND THE BOMB

With his equation $E = mc^2$, Einstein established that small amounts of matter could theoretically be converted into huge amounts of energy, but in 1905, unlocking that energy was beyond the capabilities of human technology. A few decades later, however, scientists had gained a better understanding of nuclear physics. They began researching ways to split the nucleus of an atom of a radioactive element, a process called nuclear fission.

In 1939, a physicist named Leo Szilard paid a visit to Einstein. He feared that Germany could potentially develop an extraordinarily powerful weapon using nuclear fission. Szilard, who believed that President Roosevelt would listen to the most famous scientist in the world, asked Einstein to write a letter to President Roosevelt urging him to support an American effort to develop a nuclear weapon before the Germans. Einstein's letter helped spur Roosevelt to support the Manhattan Project, which eventually succeeded in creating the atomic bomb. Einstein was never involved in the project, however, and—as a pacifist—he was horrified that the bomb was dropped on Japan in 1945.

speed of light to remain stable. He did not consider the possibility that rather than remaining stable, the object could implode. Just as Einstein was unwilling to imagine a universe in flux, he could not conceive of the notion that a star could collapse upon itself, even though the scenario was consistent with the theory of relativity.

In the late 1930s, the physicist J. Robert Oppenheimer investigated the fate of dying stars. He knew that small stars collapsed into white dwarfs, but he wondered what the theory of relativity predicted would happen when a large star ran out of fuel. The calculations showed that the star would continue collapsing and contracting indefinitely, with no end. The results were puzzling since they did not at the time describe any known object.

Black holes are difficult to detect and study because they are invisible. They warp space-time so drastically that not even light can escape their gravitational field. Therefore, they must be identified through indirect evidence.

In 1971, cosmologists identified the celestial object Cygnus X-1—a source of cosmic X-rays flashing through

In an artist's conception, the black hole Cygnus X-1 orbits its blue giant companion star and captures a stream of gas that flows from the star's atmosphere.

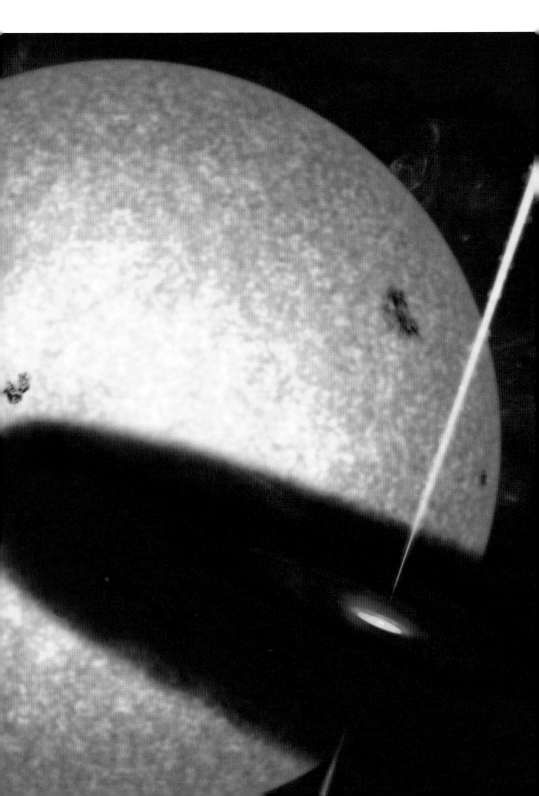

space—as a black hole. Scientists have determined that Cygnus X-1 is a binary star consisting of a blue giant closely orbited by a black hole that formed from the collapse of a massive star millions of years ago. The black hole, which has an event horizon spinning so fast that it makes more than eight hundred revolutions a second, pulls gas away from the companion star. The gas falling toward the black hole is heated to such high temperatures that it generates X-rays.

The 1919 Solar Eclipse

In 1919, Einstein had the opportunity to prove the validity of his general theory of relativity to the world in a dramatic demonstration. He had suggested as early as 1907 that a gravitational field could bend light. Even before he finalized his general theory, a group of German astronomers had made an unsuccessful attempt to test his prediction. In 1914, they traveled to make observations of a solar eclipse that was visible in Russia. During the expedition, World War I broke out and the astronomers were detained as prisoners of war.

The solar eclipse of 1919, which occurred on May 29, was visible only in the Southern Hemisphere between

South America and Africa. Arthur Eddington, a British astronomer, volunteered to lead an expedition near the equator to make observations. Eddington, an early supporter of Einstein's general theory of relativity, had been one of the first scientists to describe the theory in English. The expedition set sail in early March and split up into two groups. One team of astronomers made their observations in northern Brazil, the other from a small island off the Atlantic coast of Africa.

Arthur Eddington led the 1919 expedition that offered proof of Einstein's theory of general relativity, later writing a book entitled *Mathematical Theory of Relativity*.

The two groups planned to photograph the eclipse, in which the sun was surrounded by a group of stars. Relativity predicted that the light from the stars should be pulled toward the sun by the curvature of space-time. The effect would be greater for stars in the group that were closer to the sun. The amount of deflection would be determined

by comparing the eclipse photo to a photo of the same group of stars taken at night. If the positions of the stars varied from one photo to another, it would prove the predictions made by relativity.

The British expedition to Brazil yielded photographs showing the position of the stars adjacent to the sun during the May 29, 1919, eclipse.

The experiment not only tested Einstein's theory, it pitted the predictions made by relativity directly against Newton's theories. Because Newton considered light a particle, his theories allowed for the possibility that gravity could deflect light. But the deflection predicted by Newton's equations was only half the amount of the deflection predicted by general relativity. Therefore, the eclipse would yield no deflection or a small deflection—both compatible with Newton's physics—or Einstein's larger deflection.

The astronomers' efforts were complicated by uncooperative weather and malfunctioning equipment, but the groups managed to obtain several photographs. After the eclipse, the astronomers had to travel back home before the photos could be developed and analyzed.

The results were not released until autumn. Eddington used the best-quality photos for his calculations, and he found that the measurement of deflection confirmed the predictions made by Einstein's general theory of relativity.

Headlines across the world announced the findings as a revelation in science. A *New York Times* headline claimed that "Men of Science More or Less Agog Over Results of Eclipse Observations." Einstein became instantly famous. His book on relativity, translated into English, became a best seller.

PUTTING RELATIVITY TO THE TEST

Chapter 6

S pace-time is undetectable. It is not possible to glimpse the curvature of a gravitational field with a telescope or measure it with a space probe. The evidence supporting Einstein's theory comes from indirect observations that confirm the predictions of general relativity. Some of Einstein's predictions were proven experimentally during his lifetime, and scientists have continued to build on his legacy. For example, Einstein demonstrated how the curvature of space-time around the sun affects the orbit of Mercury. Recent computer simulations analyzing Mercury's planetary motion, taking general relativity into consideration, reveal a tiny chance that in about 3.3 billion years it could collide with one of the other inner planets of the solar system.

Technological advances have provided modern scientists the means to verify other effects of relativity decades and even nearly a century after Einstein produced his theory. In addition, new discoveries and innovations in physics and astronomy throughout the twentieth and twenty-first centuries have proven consistent with the framework of the universe based on general relativity.

Einstein, however, retreated from some of the scientific advances made possible by his own work. He did not believe in the existence of black holes and he was resistant to the idea of the universe having its origins in the big bang. He also rejected the ramifications of quantum mechanics even though he had made important contributions early on in the field.

Einstein won the 1921 Nobel Prize for Physics, however, he did not officially receive the award until the following year, and it was not for his theory of relativity, which was still considered controversial. Instead, Einstein was awarded the prize for his work

By 1920, Einstein was world famous and found himself deluged with requests and invitations. Here is a 1921 artist portrait of Einstein at work.

on the photoelectric effect. In his 1923 lecture, Einstein spoke about relativity, not the photoelectric effect. (He did not attend the 1922 Nobel ceremony, but this is widely considered Einstein's acceptance speech.) He also described his newest pursuit, the creation of a unified field theory that would reconcile his own theory of relativity with electromagnetism.

Einstein left Germany in 1932 as the Nazi regime came to power in Germany. He settled in the United States, taking a position at the Institute for Advanced Study in Princeton, New Jersey. For the rest of his life, his primary focus was his quest for a unified field theory, and he ultimately failed to produce a completed version.

The Accelerating Universe

In 1923, astronomer Edwin Hubble made observations of the Andromeda Nebula with a new telescope at the Mount Wilson Observatory, then the largest in the world. He realized that the object was not a cloud of gas, as believed, but a separate galaxy—the Andromeda galaxy. The Milky Way was only one of billions of galaxies throughout the universe. Using observations of a type of star called Cepheid variables, Hubble could determine

QUANTUM GRAVITY

Einstein spent the last years of his life unsuccessfully attempting to craft a unified field theory that would refute the principles of quantum mechanics, the discipline of physics dealing with interactions of energy and matter on the subatomic scale. Today, although both quantum mechanics and general relativity have been accepted as valid, the two theories are incompatible. Some physicists have attempted to reconcile quantum mechanics and general relativity, such as by developing a model for quantum gravity. The detection of primordial gravitational waves in 2014 could conceivably provide a link between the two theories. The gravitational waves—compatible with general relativity—were generated during the early inflation of the universe, during which interactions occurred on the scale dealt with in quantum mechanics.

the distance of some newly discovered galaxies from Earth.

When Einstein produced his model of the universe in 1917, he had added the cosmological constant to keep it stable. Other physicists, however, came up with their own models using Einstein's equations. In 1928, Hubble met with Willem de Sitter, a Dutch

physicist who had devised a model of an expanding universe. De Sitter predicted that galaxies moving away from Earth could be identified by changes in the wavelengths in the spectra of their light, a phenomenon called redshift. Hubble began analyzing the spectra of the galaxies he had observed.

In 1929, Hubble announced that his observations proved that the universe was expanding. He had found that the greater the distance of a galaxy from Earth, the faster it was moving away. Galaxies were moving apart from each other across the universe. In 1931, Einstein visited Hubble at his observatory and acknowledged that he had been wrong in his insistence of a static universe. In a new edition of his book on relativity, he added an appendix repudiating the cosmological constant.

If the galaxies of the universe were moving outward, it implied that the universe was expanding from some initial point of origin. The universe had a beginning. Physicists began to speculate that the universe had been created from a small singularity that rapidly expanded outward. In 1949, this model was dubbed the big bang theory. The theory was consistent with

Astronomer Edwin Hubble is shown before the telescope at the Mount Wilson Observatory, where his observations of galaxies changed how humans view the universe.

Hubble made observations of the Andromeda galaxy, Earth's nearest galactic neighbor, which is predicted to collide with the Milky Way galaxy in about four billion years.

general relativity, although Einstein was reluctant to support the idea.

In the mid-1960s, two scientists working for Bell Labs had an opportunity to use a radio telescope for astronomical research. In preparing the telescope, however, they could not get rid of a persistent background noise in their results. While they were attempting to fix the problem, a colleague attended a lecture by a Princeton scientist who theorized that

remnant radiation from the big bang still permeated space. It was eventually confirmed that the background hiss was cosmic microwave background radiation, which provided the first experimental evidence of the big bang.

Einstein had discarded his cosmological constant in the 1920s. Recent research, however, has shown that the concept of an adjustment factor might prove relevant yet again in the most recent models of the universe.

Although Hubble and other astronomers had proven that the universe was expanding, they had no way of determining the rate of expansion. They

had used Cepheid variable stars to determine the distances of galaxies, but these stars could only be used for short distances. To learn more about the history of the universe, scientists needed a means of determining much longer distances.

In the 1990s, scientists made observations of a certain type of supernova—an exploding star—briefly

In 1994, a supernova exploded in the spiral galaxy NGC 3370. It belonged to a subclass of supernova that can be used to chart the rate of expansion of the universe.

visible for vast distances across the cosmos. They expected to find that the rate of expansion of the universe would be gradually slowing because of gravitational fields. Instead, they were shocked to find that the expansion rate was increasing.

In his model, Einstein had intended the cosmological constant to represent a repulsive effect that would counteract the force of gravity, thus maintaining stability and preventing expansion. After discovering that the universe is expanding at an increasing rate, the concept of a repulsive form of gravity became useful once again. Scientists have come to believe that the repulsive effect is caused by the presence of "dark energy" permeating space. In recent cosmological models, dark energy makes up about 68 percent of the universe, a substance called dark matter makes up about 27 percent, and ordinary matter makes up only about 5 percent.

PROBING THE COSMOS

Technology has gradually caught up with many of the predictions made by the general theory of relativity. Space-time cannot be studied directly, and the effects of gravitational fields on space-time are often subtle or distant. The idea behind one project designed to prove Einstein's predictions—Gravity Probe B—was first proposed in 1963. It took decades of research, testing, and preparation before the spacecraft was launched in 2004. Many of Einstein's predictions remained theoretical until after his death.

While developing his general theory of relativity, Einstein had considered the possibility that not only could gravity bend light, but curved space-time could function like a lens. He set the idea aside until the 1930s, when an engineer urged him to explore the concept further. Einstein eventually published a paper titled "Lens-like Action of a Star by Deviation of Light in the Gravitational Field." He considered the phenomenon of little practical use and doubted that it would ever be observed experimentally.

Gravitational lensing, as it is now called, occurs when a huge celestial object such as a galaxy or black hole falls directly between the observer and another distant object. The gravitational field of the galaxy acts upon the image of the faraway object in ways analogous to the effects of a telescope lens. The image can be distorted, weakened, or magnified. Often, the gravitational lens creates repeated images as the light from the distant object diverges into two or more paths around the galaxy.

The first instance of geographical lensing was observed in the late 1970s, when astronomers spotted two identical quasars, bright cores of faraway galaxies, in close proximity. They concluded that it was a double image of a single quasar, and the repeated image was created by gravitational lensing. Today, gravitational lenses are a valuable tool for observing far distant objects. The Hubble Space

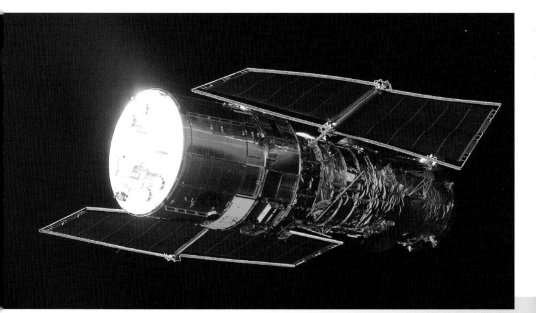

The Hubble Space Telescope, launched in 1990, is sometimes aided by naturally occurring gravitational lenses created by massive objects that bend the fabric of space-time.

Telescope has used the gravitational lensing effect as a "zoom lens" for observing some of the youngest galaxies ever glimpsed.

Yet another effect predicted by the theory of relativity is known as gravitational redshift. Hubble observed one type of redshift resulting from cosmological expansion. A gravitational field can also cause a redshift, although the effect is much smaller. Gravitational redshift was first detected in a 1959 experiment involving gamma rays, which are also subject to the effect since they are a type of electromagnetic radiation. Harvard researchers measured the wavelengths of gamma rays emitted by radioactive iron, and then remeasured them after they had fallen a distance of 73.8 feet (22.5 m). The wavelengths at the bottom registered a very slight redshift, confirming the predictions made by general relativity. Redshift has also been observed astronomically in the light emitted by faraway clusters of galaxies.

In the early 2000s, a space experiment called Gravity Probe B confirmed two more fundamental predictions of general relativity. The spacecraft carried four highly precise instruments called gyroscopes that spin on an axis. The gyroscopes were pointed at a single star, but over the course of the experiment, the direction of their spin shifted slightly due to the effect of Earth's gravity on space and time. The experiment confirmed the warping of space-time around Earth, known as the geodetic effect. It also found that Earth pulls space-time around with it during rotation, known as the frame-dragging effect.

ECHOES FROM THE BIG BANG

In March 2014, the news flashed across the world that scientists had observed gravitational waves generated shortly after the big bang. The finding confirmed a key prediction of the general theory of relativity and provided a glimpse into the first trillionth of a trillionth of a trillionth of a second after the creation of the universe.

Einstein predicted the existence of gravitational waves in 1916. A massive disturbance involving acceleration, such as two black holes colliding, could cause shock waves of gravity rippling through the fabric of space at the speed of light. The effect would be very faint, and Einstein did not believe that they would ever be detected experimentally.

In 1974, astronomers achieved the first indirect detection of gravitational waves when observing a system of two stars locked in close orbit. At least one of the stars was a pulsar, a dense star emitting bursts of energy. The scientists monitored the star and determined that it was gradually slowing down. The slowdown was consistent with the prediction that the pulsar was producing gravitational waves.

The 2014 discovery of the primordial gravitational waves was made by a radio telescope at the South Pole called BICEP 2 (Background Imaging of Cosmic Extragalactic Polarization 2). The telescope scans the sky for evidence of the cosmic microwave background radiation left over from the big bang. The signature can be seen on a polarization map as swirls representing polarized light waves, the result of gravitational waves stretching and squeezing space as they travel. The finding is the most direct confirmation of Einstein's theory, and it is also the first time that gravitational waves have been observed affecting matter other than their own source.

Notably, the gravitational waves confirm a theory called inflation, which hypothesizes that the universe underwent an incredibly massive expansion during the first few very brief moments of its existence. The huge amounts of energy propelled outward during the inflation produced the gravitational waves still detectible in the cosmic microwave background radiation. The discovery of gravitational waves represents a significant breakthrough in understanding the earliest evolution of the universe.

Located at a South Pole research station, the South Pole Telescope and BICEP (Background Imaging of Cosmic Extragalactic Polarization) collect data on cosmic microwave background radiation.

Einstein's general theory of relativity has long been established as a cornerstone of the field of cosmology, yet the outcomes of his theory are still fresh and exciting to this day. Throughout his life, Einstein tended to pursue sweeping theories that would reconcile contradictions or unify separate disciplines of physics. It is entirely fitting that in the twenty-first century, Einstein's theoretical framework continues to be applied to questions about the origin and the fundamental nature of the universe.

1632 Galileo Galilei is the first to describe relativity of motion.

1687 Sir Isaac Newton's *Philosophiae Naturalis Principia Mathematica* (*Mathematical Principles of Natural Philosophy*) presents three laws of motion.

1887 Albert Michelson and Edward Morley design the interferometer, hoping to detect the presence of ether.

1900 Max Planck suggests that energy exists in bundles called quanta.

1905 Albert Einstein presents his theory of the nature of light and the photoelectric effect. Einstein expands Planck's theory and proposes that light is made up of quanta, which could be represented as a wave.
In his paper "A New Determination of Molecular Dimensions" Einstein confirms the size of sugar molecules.
Einstein proves the existence of atoms.
Einstein publishes the paper that introduces the famous equation $E = mc^2$.

1906 Max Planck is the first scientist to publish an article in support of the theory of relativity.

1907 Einstein has the "happiest moment of his life," which leads to the principle of equivalence and an explanation of the relationship between inertia, gravity, and acceleration.

1908 Hermann Minkowski introduces the formulation of four-dimensional space-time.

1915 Einstein presents the general theory of relativity to the world.

1919 A solar eclipse provides Einstein with the data he needs to verify his theory of relativity.

1921 Einstein wins the Nobel Prize for Physics.

1923 Edwin Hubble discovers the Andromeda galaxy.

1929 Hubble announces that his observations prove that the universe is expanding.

1949 Hubble's model is named the big bang theory.

1959 Gravitational redshift is first observed.

1963 Gravity Probe B is proposed.

1971 Cosmologists identify Cygnus X-1 as a black hole.

1974 Astronomers attain the first indirect detection of gravitational waves.

2004 Gravity Probe B is launched.

2014 Primordial gravitational waves are detected, making a possible link between quantum mechanics and general relativity theories.

acceleration The rate of change in an object's velocity.

black hole An object so dense that not even light can escape its gravity.

celestial Positioned in or relating to outer space.

cosmology The study of the origin, evolution, structure, and eventual fate of the universe.

field A region surrounding an object in which a force is exerted on other objects.

force A dynamic influence that causes a change in the motion of an object.

general relativity Einstein's 1915 theory explaining gravity as the curvature of space-time.

inertia An object's resistance to change in its motion.

inflation In cosmology, the early rapid expansion of the universe.

orbit The gravitationally curved path of an object in space.

paradox A statement or proposition that leads to a logically unacceptable conclusion despite sound reasoning and analysis.

principle of equivalence Einstein's statement that it is impossible to distinguish the effects of gravity from the effects of acceleration.

quantum mechanics Also called quantum physics and quantum theory, the discipline of physics dealing with interactions of energy and matter on the subatomic scale.

radiation The emission of energy as electromagnetic waves or particles.

redshift A shift of spectral lines of a celestial object toward the red end of the spectrum, usually caused by the object moving further away.

singularity A region in which the theories of mathematics and physics break down, for example, the center of a black hole.

space-time The four-dimensional system of coordinates including three physical dimensions combined with time.

special relativity Einstein's 1905 theory based on the principles that the laws of physics are the same for all inertial frames of reference and that the speed of light is constant.

velocity A measure of an object's rate of motion that takes into account both speed and direction.

wavelength The distance between two peaks or valleys of a wave.

American Institute of Physics (AIP)
One Physics Ellipse
College Park, MD 20740
(301) 209-3100
Website: http://www.aip.org
AIP serves a federation of physical science societ-
ies in a common mission to promote physics and
allied fields.

Canada Science and Technology Museum
1867 St Laurent Blvd
Ottawa, Ontario K1G 5A3
Canada
(613) 991-3044
Website: http://www.sciencetech.technomuses.ca
The Canada Science and Technology Museums
Corporation aims to help the public to under-
stand the ongoing relationships between
science, technology, and Canadian society.

Canadian Association of Physicists (CAP)
Suite 112, MacDonald Building
University of Ottawa
150 Louis Pasteur Priv.
Ottawa, Ontario K1N 6N5
Canada
(613) 562-5614

Website: http://www.cap.ca
The Canadian Association of Physicists works to
    highlight achievements in Canadian physics and
    to pursue scientific, educational, public policy,
    and communication initiatives that enhance the
    vitality of the discipline.

Einstein Museum
Helvetiaplatz 5
CH-3005 Bern
Switzerland
+41 31 350 77 11
Website: http://www.bhm.ch/en/exhibitions/
    einstein-museum
Affiliated with the Historical Museum of Bern
    (Bernisches Historisches Museum), the Einstein
    Museum is dedicated to the life and work of
    Albert Einstein.

Institute for Advanced Study (IAS)
Einstein Drive
Princeton, NJ 08540
(609) 734-8000
Website: http://www.ias.edu
The institution where Einstein taught after immi-
    grating to the United States, the Institute for
    Advanced Study is one of the world's leading

centers for theoretical research and intellectual inquiry.

Mt. Wilson Observatory
466 Foothill Blvd, #327
La Canada, CA 91011
(626) 440-9016
Website: http://www.mtwilson.edu
The observatory where Hubble made his observations of the expanding universe, Mt. Wilson Observatory is now open to the public.

WEBSITES

Because of the changing nature of Internet links, Rosen Publishing has developed an online list of websites related to the subject of this book. This site is updated regularly. Please use this link to access the list:

http://www.rosenlinks.com/PHYS/Rela

Calaprice, Alice. *The Ultimate Quotable Einstein.* Princeton, NJ: Princeton University Press, 2011.

Couper, Heather. *Encyclopedia of Space.* New York, NY: DK Publishing, 2009.

Cox, Brian. *Why Does E=mc² (and Why Should We Care?).* Cambridge, MA: Da Capo Press, 2010.

Forman, Lillian E. *Albert Einstein: Physicist and Genius.* Edina, MN: ABDO Publishing, 2009.

Gregersen, Erik, ed. *The Britannica Guide to Relativity and Quantum Mechanics.* New York, NY: Britannica Educational Publishing, 2011.

Herweck, Don. *Albert Einstein and His Theory of Relativity.* Mankato, MN: Compass Point Books, 2009.

Hollihan, Kerrie Logan. *Isaac Newton and Physics for Kids: His Life and Ideas with 21 Activities.* Chicago, IL: Chicago Review Press, 2009.

Holzner, Steven. *Physics for Dummies,* 2nd ed. Hoboken, NJ: Wiley, 2011.

Holzner, Steven. *Quantum Physics for Dummies.* Hoboken, NJ: Wiley, 2013.

Karam, P. Andrew. *Matter and Energy.* New York, NY: Chelsea House, 2011.

Lew, Kristi. *The Expanding Universe.* New York, NY: Chelsea House, 2011.

Lightman, Alan. *Einstein's Dreams.* New York, NY: Vintage, 2004.

Manning, Phillip. *Gravity*. New York, NY: Chelsea House, 2011.

Manning, Phillip. *Quantum Theory*. New York, NY: Chelsea House, 2011.

Krull, Kathleen. *Albert Einstein*. New York, NY: Viking, 2009.

Parker, Katie. *The Theory of Relativity*. Tarrytown, NY: Marshall Cavendish Benchmark, 2010.

Perricone, Mike. *The Big Bang*. New York, NY: Chelsea House, 2009.

Pickover, Clifford. *The Physics Book: From the Big Bang to Quantum Resurrection: 250 Milestones in the History of Physics*. New York, NY: Sterling, 2011.

Pohlen, Jerome. *Albert Einstein and Relativity for Kids: His Life and Ideas with 21 Activities and Thought Experiments*. Chicago, IL: Chicago Review Press, 2012.

Rosen, Joe. *Encyclopedia of Physical Science*. New York, NY: Facts on File, 2010.

Scott, Elaine. *Space, Stars, and the Beginning of Time: What the Hubble Telescope Saw*. Boston, MA: Clarion Books, 2011.

Bryner, Jeanna. "Long Shot: Planet Could Hit Earth in Distant Future." Space.com, June 10, 2009. Retrieved May 10, 2014 (http://www.space .com/6824-long-shot-planet-hit-earth-distant -future.html).

Calle, Carlos I. *Einstein for Dummies*. Hoboken, NJ: Wiley Publishing, 2005.

Carlisle, Camille M. "Direct Evidence of Big Bang Inflation." *Sky and Telescope*, March 17, 2014.

Cassidy, David C. *Einstein and Our World*, 2nd ed. Amherst, NY: Humanity Books, 2004.

Einstein, Albert. *Relativity*. New York, NY: Prometheus Books, 1995.

Eisenstaedt, Jean. *The Curious History of Relativity: How Einstein's Theory of Gravity Was Lost and Found Again*. Princeton, NJ: Princeton University Press, 2006.

Ferraro, Rafael. *Einstein's Space-Time: An Introduction to Special and General Relativity*. New York, NY: Springer, 2007.

Greene, Brian. "Darkness on the Edge of the Universe." *New York Times*, January 15, 2011.

Isaacson, Walter. *Einstein: His Life and Universe*. New York, NY: Simon and Schuster, 2007.

Manning, Phillip. *Theory of Relativity*. New York, NY: Chelsea House, 2011.

Kaku, Michio. *Einstein's Cosmos: How Albert Einstein's Vision Transformed Our*

Understanding of Space and Time. New York, NY: Atlas Books, 2004.

Orzel, Chad. *How to Teach Relativity to Your Dog.* New York, NY: Basic Books, 2012.

Overbye, Dennis. "Space Ripples Reveal Big Bang's Smoking Gun." *New York Times*, March 17, 2014.

Parker, Barry. *Einstein's Brainchild: Relativity Made Relatively Easy!* New York, NY: Prometheus Books, 2000.

Perrotto, Trent J. "NASA's Gravity Probe B Confirms Two Einstein Space-Time Theories." NASA, May 4, 2011. Retrieved May 10, 2014 (http://www.nasa.gov/mission_pages/gpb /gpb_results.html).

Rigdon, John S. *Einstein 1905: The Standard of Greatness.* Cambridge, MA: Harvard University Press, 2005.

Rindler, Wolfgang. *Relativity: Special, General, and Cosmological,* 2nd ed. New York, NY: Oxford University Press, 2006.

Robinson, Andrew. *Einstein: A Hundred Years of Relativity.* New York, NY: Harry N. Abrams, 2005.

"Scientific Background on the Nobel Prize in Physics 2011: The Accelerating Universe." The Royal Swedish Academy of Sciences, October 4, 2011. Retrieved May 10, 2014 (http://www.nobelprize

.org/nobel_prizes/physics/laureates/2011
/advanced-physicsprize2011.pdf).

Wolfson, Richard. *Simply Einstein: Relativity Demystified*. New York, NY: W. W. Norton and Company, 2003.

A

atomic bomb, Einstein and, 71

B

big bang theory, 80, 85–87, 93
black holes, 7, 64, 69–74, 80, 90, 93
Brown, Robert, 27
Brownian motion, 27–29

C

"Cosmological Considerations in the General Theory of Relativity," 67
cosmological constant, 67, 83, 85, 87, 89
cosmology, general relativity and, 63–78, 79–80, 83, 86, 90, 92, 93, 94, 95
covariance, principle of, 57
Cygnus X-1, 72–74

D

dark energy, 89
dark matter, 89

"Does the Inertia of a Body Depend on Its Energy Content?" 42

E

Eddington, Arthur, 5–6, 75, 78
E=mc² equation, 26, 41, 42–45, 71
Einstein, Albert
    and the atomic bomb, 71
    early life of, 20–31
    and general theory of relativity, 4–7, 46–62, 63–78, 79–80, 83, 86, 90, 92, 93, 94, 95
    marriages of, 24, 63–64
    and Nobel Prize for Physics, 80–82
    as a pacifist, 63, 71
    papers of 1905, 25–29, 31, 32, 44
    and special theory of relativity, 6–7, 32–45, 48, 52, 57
Einstein: A Hundred Years of Relativity, 5, 9
Einstein: His Life and Universe, 31, 42, 43, 62
Einstein 1905, 35
equivalence, principle of, 49–52, 57, 65
ether, 8, 18–19, 33, 47

Euclidian geometry, 53–54, 57
event horizon, 70, 74

F

FitzGerald, George Francis, 37
"Foundation of the General Theory of Relativity, The," 64
frame-dragging effect, 93

G

Galileo Galilei, 9–11, 33
general theory of relativity, 4–7, 46–62
  and celestial objects/ cosmology, 63–78, 79–80, 83, 86, 90, 92, 93, 94, 95
geodetic effect, 93
global positioning system (GPS), 58
gravitational lensing, 90–92
gravitational redshift, 92
gravity, as curved space-time, 7, 55–59
gravity, Newton's law of, 12–13, 55, 65, 70
Gravity Probe B, 90, 92

H

Hawking, Stephen, 5
Hubble, Edwin, 82–85, 87

I

inflation, 94
interferometer, 18
Isaacson, Walter, 31, 42, 43, 62

L

length contraction, 36–37
"Lens-like Action of a Star by Deviation of Light in the Gravitational Field," 90
light
  nature of, 15–19, 26–27
  quantum theory of, 27
  speed of, 33–35, 40–42, 44, 45, 47, 65
Lorentz, Hendrik, 37, 38
Lorentz transformations, 38
Löwenthal, Elsa, 64

M

Manhattan Project, 71
Marić, Mileva, 23, 24, 26, 63–64

Maxwell, James Clerk, 15–18, 33, 42, 44

Maxwell's equations, 17, 33, 42

Mercury, and Einstein's theory, 59–62, 79–80

Michell, John, 70

Michelson, Albert, 18–19, 23

Minkowski, Hermann, 52–53

Morley, Edward, 18–19, 23

motion, Newton's laws of, 11–12, 13–15, 49, 59, 61

N

"New Determination of Molecular Dimensions, A," 27

Newton, Isaac, 11–15, 27, 35, 49, 55, 57, 59, 61, 65, 70, 77

Nobel Prize for Physics, 80–82

O

"On the Electrodynamics of Moving Bodies," 32

"On the Investigation of the State of Ether in a Magnetic Field," 22

Oppenheimer, J. Robert, 72

"Outline of a Generalized Theory of Relativity and a Theory of Gravitation," 59

P

particle accelerators, 41

photoelectric effect, 26, 82

Planck, Max, 26, 46–47

Poincaré, Henri, 37

Principia, 11

Q

quanta, 26

quantum gravity, 83

quantum mechanics, 27, 80, 83

R

redshift, 85, 92

Relativity: The Special and the General Theory, 64

Riemann, Bernhard, 54, 57

Rigdon, John S., 35

Robinson, Andrew, 5, 9

Roosevelt, President, 71

S

Schwarzschild, Karl, 67–70
Schwarzschild radius, 69–70
Schwarzschild
    singularities, 70
singularity, 70, 85
Sitter, Willem de, 83–85
solar eclipse of 1919, 64,
    74–78
special theory of
    relativity, 6–7,
    32–45, 48, 52, 57
Szilard, Leo, 71

T

tensors, 54, 59, 61
time dilation, 36, 37
twin paradox, 38–40

U

unified field theory, 82, 83
universe, expansion of, 7,
    64, 85–89

V

vectors, 54

W

World War I, 63, 74

Z

Zurich, University of, 27, 48
Zurich Polytechnic Institute,
    22, 23, 24, 52, 54

ABOUT THE AUTHOR

Corona Brezina has written more than a dozen young-adult books for Rosen Publishing. Several of her previous books have also focused on topics related to science and the environment, including *The Laws of Thermodynamics* and *In the News: Climate Change*. She lives in Chicago.

PHOTO CREDITS

Cover Zap Art/Photographer's Choice/Getty Images; p. 4 © iStockphoto.com/DSGpro; pp. 6, 54, 76–77 Science & Society Picture Library/Getty Images; pp. 10, 47 Science Source/Photo Researchers/Getty Images; p. 11 De Agostini Picture Library/Getty Images; pp. 12–13 Reto Stöckli, Nazmi El Saleous, Marit Jentoft-Nilsen/NASA/GSFC; p. 16 Photodisc/Thinkstock; p. 19 Museum of Science and Industry, Chicago/Getty Images; p. 21 Print Collector/Hulton Archive/Getty Images; p. 25 © SZ Photo/Scherl/The Image Works; pp. 28–29 Ted Kinsman/Science Source; p. 30 Topical Press Agency/Hulton Archive/Getty Images; p. 34 Grant Faint/The Image Bank/Getty Images; p. 37 Royal Astronomical Society/Science Source; p. 39 laskvv/iStock/Thinkstock; pp. 42–43 Johnny Eggitt/AFP/Getty Images; pp. 50, 56, 88–89, 91 NASA; p. 53 akg-images/Newscom; p. 60 NASA/Johns Hopkins University Applied Physics Laboratory/Carnegie Institution; p. 68 Emilio Segrè Visual Archives/American Institute of Physics/Science Source; p. 73 Stocktrek Images/Getty Images; p. 75 Science and Society/SuperStock; p. 81 Heritage Images/Hulton Archive/Getty Images; p. 84 Jean-Leon Huens/National Geographic Image Collection/Getty Images; pp. 86–87 NASA/JPL-Caltech; p. 95 Nick Powell/National Science Foundation; cover and interior design elements Shutterstock.com.

Designer: Les Kanturek; Editor: Heather Moore Niver